Dominoes
AROUND THE WORLD

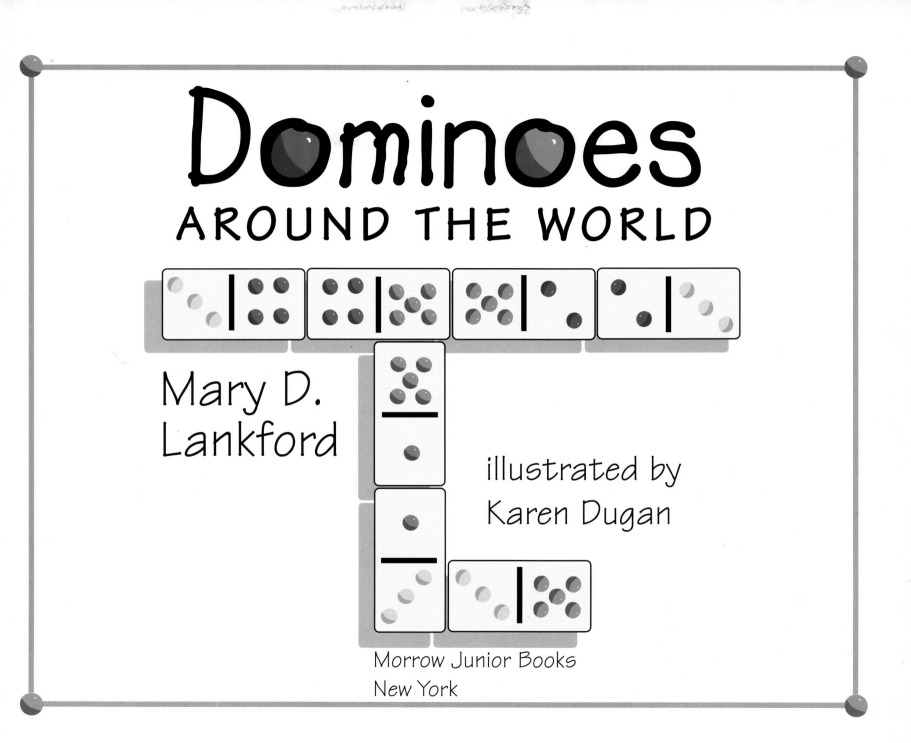

Mary D. Lankford

illustrated by
Karen Dugan

Morrow Junior Books
New York

1 Cuba

2 France

3 Malta

4 The Netherlands

5 Spain

6 Ukraine

7 United States

8 Vietnam

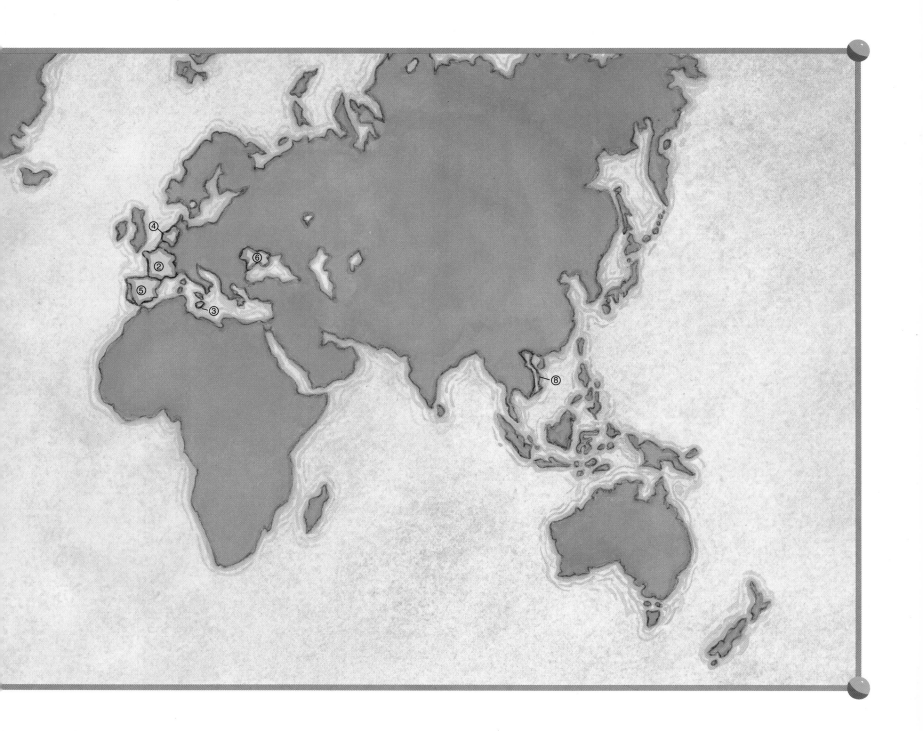

For Grant Walker Jordan
who continues to be a splendid idea
and
Lynnette Lankford Jordan
who had the idea for both Grant and this book
—M.D.L.

Acknowledgments

With each book I research and write, I continue to be indebted to people who give freely of their time and their interest, and who add immeasurably to the quality of the final publication. Listing these names seems a very small reward for assisting in the development of this book; however, this must suffice. The assistance is always appreciated. I hope none of those who should be acknowledged is omitted. Special thanks to Pam Pollack, New York; Sue Flemmons, Irving, Texas, for Mexican Train; Sylvia Mora Mavrogenes, Miami Public Library, Ondina Arrondo, Hispanic Library, Miami, Florida, and Ralph De La Cruz, Los Angeles, California, for Cuban Dominoes; Dr. Valeria Kukharenko, for Ukrainian Dominoes; Steve Raymen, for searching for books in England and providing good reference materials; and Thu Le, University of Dallas, for Vietnamese Dominoes. Always a debt of gratitude to John Briley and Meredith Charpentier for their support and guidance.

Published by Morrow Junior Books
a division of William Morrow and Company, Inc.
1350 Avenue of the Americas, New York, NY 10019
http://www.williammorrow.com

Printed in Hong Kong
1 2 3 4 5 6 7 8 9 10

Library of Congress Cataloging-in-Publication Data
Lankford, Mary D.
Dominoes around the world/by Mary D. Lankford; illustrated by Karen Dugan.
p. cm.
Includes index.
Summary: Examines the history and basic rules of the game of dominoes and describes how it can vary from country to country.
ISBN 0-688-14051-3 (trade)—ISBN 0-688-14052-1 (library)
1. Dominoes—Juvenile literature. [1. Dominoes.] I. Dugan, Karen, ill. II. Title.
GV1467.L36 1998 795.3'2—dc21 97-20975 CIP AC

Watercolors, gouache, and colored pencils were used for the full-color illustrations.
The text type is 13.5-point Tekton.
Book design by Trish Parcell Watts.

Contents

Playing Dominoes 6

Looking over the Bones 8

Fundamentals of Play 10

Cuban Dominoes **Cuba** 12

French Draw **France** 14

Maltese Cross **Malta** 16

Bergen **The Netherlands** 18

Matador **Spain** 20

Ukrainian Dominoes **Ukraine** 22

Blind Hughie **United States** 24

Mexican Train **United States** 26

Muggins **United States** 28

Vietnamese Dominoes **Vietnam** 30

Dominoes for One Player 32

Domino Puzzles 35

Delectable Disappearing Dominoes 37

Domino Dictionary 38

Bibliography 39

Index 40

Playing Dominoes

When I hear the clicking sound of dominoes being shuffled, dealt, or tapped together as players wait their turn, it brings back memories of family reunions and the laughter of friends. My childhood game was played sitting beneath a card table, while above us the adults played more complicated games of their own. The faces of our old-fashioned wooden dominoes were black with white spots, decorated on the back with a raised design of an eagle or a crown. Today most dominoes are made from plastic, and dominoes come in standard, professional, and tournament sizes.

My curiosity about the origins of childhood games led me to write *Hopscotch Around the World* and *Jacks Around the World*. The idea for a book about dominoes came from a newspaper article sent to me by my daughter, Lynnette Jordan, a librarian in Houston, Texas. The article described a company in Waco, Texas, that manufactures one hundred thousand sets of dominoes every year—dominoes decorated with school colors, animals, state flags, even a player's name.

I began to wonder about the origins of the word *domino*, when and where the game began, and whether people around the world played domino games similar to the ones I knew. I learned, through research, that the game of dominoes is much older than my memories.

The domino tiles resemble those used for a game played as long ago as A.D. 1120. By the year 1400 this game, called Mah-jongg, was known all over China. It is still popular in China today.

A similar game was played in ancient Egypt. We know this because a set of dominoes was discovered when the tomb of King Tutankhamen of Egypt (1371–1352 B.C.) was opened in 1922.

A game similar to dominoes still played in the Far East is known as Kwat P'ai, which means "bone tablets," or "dotted cards." Some people believe that Venetian traders in the fourteenth or fifteenth century brought the game from China to Europe. Early game pieces were carved from wood, bone, or ivory.

Like most games, dominoes had its beginnings in ancient history and probably evolved from games played with dice, which are still used in many games. In fact, a domino is sometimes called a *bone,* and a slang term for dice is *bones.* Dominoes are similar to dice in that each pattern of spots on the end of a domino, except the blank, has a match on the face of a die, from one spot to six. Looking at a single domino is like looking at one of the possible tosses of a pair of dice.

Domino is actually a French word that originally described the hooded cloak, possibly lined in white, worn by priests. When the word *domino* traveled from France to England during the Napoleonic Wars, the meaning changed to describe a hooded masquerade costume worn with a small mask, then to describe the mask itself. If you look at the double-one domino, you can see the resemblance to the black mask. Possibly this is how the game got its name.

Another theory is that the name comes from the Latin word *dominus,* or "lord master of the house."

Dominoes, and its many variations, is still being played with rules that may have originated thousands of years ago. I am now playing dominoes with my grandchildren, just as, long ago, my grandmother did with me.

Looking over the Bones

There are twenty-eight tiles, or pieces, in a set of dominoes whose highest piece is the double-six. Sets that go up to double-nine dominoes have fifty-five tiles. Double-twelves have ninety-one. For the games in this book, a set of double-six dominoes is used.

Domino tiles are also called stones, bones, or men. The end of a domino that has no spots, or pips, is called a blank. A domino with the same number of spots on each end is called a double.

Turn all the doubles faceup, spots showing, and arrange them in a row, with the highest suit (or number of spots) first. You should have a line of seven dominoes, beginning with double-six and ending with double-blank.

Another way to get an understanding of the pieces is to turn all of the pieces faceup. Take the dominoes that have six spots on one end and arrange them in a line from highest to lowest. You should have a stack of six-six, six-five, six-four, six-three, six-two, six-one, six-blank. The second row begins with the double-five, then five-four, five-three, five-two, five-one, and five-blank. Arrange the remaining dominoes in similar rows of fours, threes, twos, and ones.

Look at the set of dominoes shown on the opposite page. There are seven suits in each set—sixes, fives, fours, threes, twos, ones, and blanks. Each of these suits has seven dominoes that match on one end. Except for doubles, the numbers on the other end are different from the suit. It is important to remember that there are seven of each number and seven blanks.

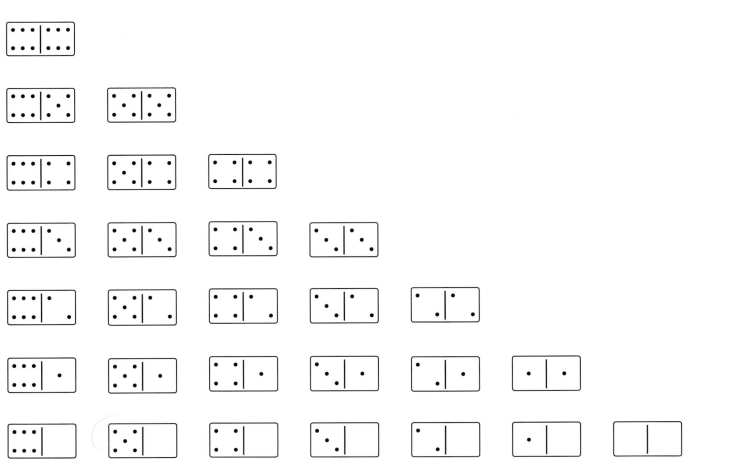

Fundamentals of Play

Before a game, dominoes are turned facedown and shuffled, or moved around, until they are mixed. Some people play that the winner of the last round also wins the right to shuffle.

Players draw dominoes from the boneyard, or bonepile—the mixed tiles lying facedown on the table. In most games, if two are playing, each player draws thirteen dominoes, leaving two in the boneyard. If three are playing, each draws nine, leaving one domino in the boneyard. And if four play, each takes six, leaving four in the boneyard.

As dominoes are drawn, they are placed in front of the player, turned on their long side. Here is a sample hand.

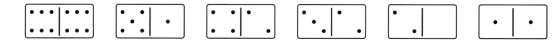

The player with the highest double goes first, placing the domino faceup in the middle of the table. The first domino played in a game is called the spinner. Here is a sample first play.

The player sitting to the left of player one goes next. She must match the end of one of the dominoes in her hand to one end of the domino already on the table. In this case, the domino must have a six on one end.

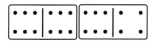

Play again moves to the left, and the third player may match either end of the line of dominoes on the table. In this case, the third player is able to play a domino with a four.

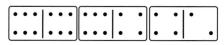

If a player does not have a domino that matches either end of the line, he draws from the boneyard until he can play. If he has drawn all the pieces in the boneyard and still can't play, his turn is over. In this case, the fourth player is able to play once he draws a domino with a six.

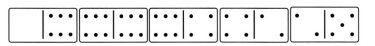

With four people, play now moves back to the player who started the game. In this case, she must match either a two on one end of the line of dominoes or a blank on the other end.

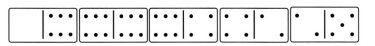

Play continues in this way until one player plays all his tiles. He calls "Domino" and is the winner. A game also ends if it becomes blocked. This occurs when no further match can be made and all dominoes have been drawn from the boneyard. If this happens, the winner of the game is the player with the lowest total number of spots on the dominoes remaining in her hand.

Many people like to play a series of rounds and keep track of points to determine an overall winner. The winner of each round takes all the points for that round. Points are determined by adding up all the spots on the dominoes the other players hold (blanks count as zero). In a blocked game, the winner subtracts his spots from this total to determine his score. Whoever is first to reach a predetermined point total—often one hundred—is the overall winner.

In all games, someone must lose. Don't get mad if you are the one. In the next game try some strategy by looking ahead at what you will be able to play. Keep in mind how many dominoes of each suit you have and watch closely to see how many dominoes of each suit have been played. Then, if you have a choice, choose to play the domino that will allow you to play when your turn comes again. Try to play a domino that starts a suit you have many of and your opponents have few of.

You can improve your memory and your thinking skills by playing dominoes, but the best reason to play this game is just to have fun.

Cuba

Cuban Dominoes

Cuba, the largest island of the West Indies, is located in the Caribbean Sea, just south of Florida. Many Cubans who have immigrated to the United States live in Miami, Florida. The weather in Cuba and Florida is mild, and the game may be played outdoors on a porch or in a park.

Cuban Dominoes is similar to the basic game described in "Fundamentals of Play." Playing Cuban Dominoes takes concentration. It is wise not to talk and slow the game. Grandparents sometimes warn children: "*El dominó lo inventó un mudo,*" or "Dominoes were invented by a person who does not talk." Everyone pays close attention to the dominoes played and attempts to make moves that block opponents from playing all their dominoes. It may look simple, but you must think fast!

How to Play:

1. Shuffle the dominoes. When two play, each draws seven dominoes. With more than two, subtract the number of players from the number eight. If there are four players, each draws four dominoes (8 - 4 = 4).

2. Player one plays any double he has. If he doesn't have one, he must draw from the boneyard until he picks up a double.

3. Player two must match one end of the double or draw.

4. Play continues until one player plays all of his dominoes, or until no one can play (blocked game) and there are no more dominoes in the boneyard.

5. The player who plays all his dominoes calls "Domino" and is the winner. The total number of spots on the other players' remaining dominoes is his score.

6. If the game is blocked, and all players are left with unplayed dominoes, the player with the smallest number of spots in his hand is the winner of the round. To determine his score, that player subtracts his spots from the total spots on the other players' dominoes. Often rounds continue until one player has reached one hundred points. That player is the overall winner.

France

French Draw France, the largest country in western Europe, has three borders on the sea: the English Channel to the north, the Bay of Biscay to the west, and the Mediterranean Sea to the south. The Alps form France's border with Italy and Switzerland, and the Pyrenees cross its border with Spain.

The game of dominoes played in this country is French Draw. France has produced many fine artists and painters, but here the word *draw* means "to choose." In this game players draw, or choose, as many dominoes as they want from the boneyard, even if they have playable dominoes in their hand. Drawing extras from the boneyard expands a player's options and may actually help the player win.

How to Play:

1. After shuffling the dominoes, two or three players draw seven dominoes each; four players draw six dominoes each.

2. Player one plays any domino from her hand.

3. Player two may match one end of the first domino played or draw as many dominoes as desired until she decides to play. Two dominoes must always remain in the boneyard.

4. Play continues around the table. Players can decide whether to play from their own hand or draw. If after drawing there is still no match, play passes to the next player.

5. The round is over when one player plays all her dominoes or when no one can play. Scoring is determined the usual way.

Malta

Maltese Cross

In the Mediterranean Sea, three small islands form a country called Malta. During the Crusades in the 1500s, the knights of King John defended Malta from invasion by the Turks. The badge of those knights, on their flag and armor, was the Maltese cross.

The shape formed by this game looks like a cross, with each of the four crossed lines capped by a crossbar. You build the cross shape as doubles are played "across the line."

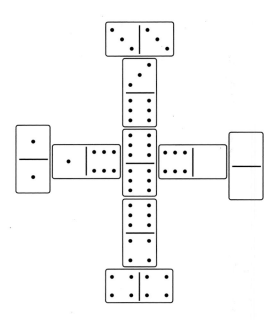

How to Play:

1. Shuffle the dominoes. Four players are needed for this game; each draws seven dominoes.

2. The player with the double-six plays first.

3. Player two must play a domino with six spots on one end. It can be played either to one of the sides or to one of the ends of the double-six.

4. Player three now plays another domino with six spots on one end, or a double that matches the other end of player two's domino. Whenever a double is played, it is played on its side, across the line.

5. The game continues with four lines radiating from the central double-six. No further dominoes can be played on a line until a double is played across the line. With every other tile having to be a double across the line, you finish the game with a shape that looks like a cross.

6. When a player cannot play, he passes. The round is over when one player plays all his dominoes or no one can play. Scoring is determined the usual way.

The Netherlands

Bergen   The northwestern European coastal country of Holland (officially called the Netherlands) has for centuries battled the North Sea. Much of the land was once covered by water. The Dutch people have built dams, dikes, and levees to reclaim almost half of the country from the North Sea.

This game might have been named after the small city of Bergen op Zoom, on the coast of the Netherlands. As the game is played, matches result in both ends of the line of dominoes having the same number of spots.

How to Play:

1. After shuffling, the two, three, or four players each draw six dominoes.

2. The player with the lowest double plays first. The first play earns a score of two points.

3. A player must match one end of the double or draw. Two dominoes must always remain in the boneyard.

4. A player scores a double header, or two points, each time she plays a domino with a spot count that matches the domino at the other end of the line.

5. A player scores a triple header, or three points, when she plays a double that matches the spot count of the domino at the other end of the line. The addition of the double-two to this line makes for a triple header.

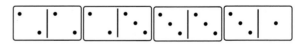

6. A player earns one point for playing all her dominoes and calling "Domino."

7. The round is over when one player plays all her dominoes or when no one can play. This game is often played up to fifteen points.

Spain

Matador Spain, or *España*, occupies most of the Iberian Peninsula, in southwestern Europe. The Pyrenees Mountains in the north extend from the Bay of Biscay to the Mediterranean Sea. In the south, Gibraltar is less than eight miles from Africa.

In Spanish-speaking countries, the bullfight is known as *la corrida de toros*, and the bullfighter is called the matador. One of the oldest domino games, played by Spaniards and others around the world, is Matador (also Russian Dominoes or All Sevens). In this game, dominoes are played so that spots on touching ends total seven, and the Matadors are wild pieces that may be played at any time and do not have to match the domino on the table. Matadors are dominoes with spots on both ends adding up to seven—for instance, a five-two domino. The double-blank is also a Matador. When a Matador is played, it is always played across the line.

How to Play:

1. Shuffle the dominoes. If two play, each player draws seven; for three, each draws six; for four, each draws five.

2. The player with the highest double goes first. With each domino played, a point is scored.

3. The spots on the end of the second player's domino and the spots on the end of the first player's domino must, when touching, total seven. For instance, if a two-two domino has been played, a domino with five spots on the end could be played on either two. A Matador may be played at any time. If two Matadors are placed next to each other, only the first one is played across the line. If playing on a Matador, the domino may match either end.

4. A player must draw from the boneyard until he can play—but a player is *not* required to play a Matador. When a player cannot play or chooses not to play a Matador, he passes.

5. The round is over when one player plays all his dominoes or when no one can play. In addition to the points scored for each domino played, the player who plays all his dominoes gets one point for each spot in his opponents' hands. If no one goes out, each player gets one point for each spot in the other players' hands, subtracting his total spots to determine his score.

Ukraine

Ukrainian Dominoes Snuggled on the edge of the Black Sea, the Ukraine is famous for its fertile farmland. Part of the former Soviet Union, the Ukraine declared independence late in 1991. Of the former republics of the Soviet Union, it is second only to Russia in population and natural resources.

Ukrainian Dominoes, or "Banging the Ivories," is often played in parks or in the courtyard of an apartment building. The game may be played on a board that leans against the wall when not being used for dominoes. Groups gather to watch, and neighbors sometimes call out the window to complain about the noise of banging tiles!

How to Play:

1. After shuffling, the two, three, or four players each draw six dominoes.

2. The player with the highest double goes first.

3. Player two must match one end of the double or draw.

4. A player must draw from the boneyard—known in the Ukraine as "going to the market"—until she can play.

5. The round is over when one player plays all her dominoes or when no one can play. Scoring is determined the usual way.

Blind Hughie

Blind Hughie is also called Billiton and Blind Dominoes. The name Billiton may have come from the island Belitung, off the shore of Sumatra. This is a game of luck, and dominoes are played as they are turned over. You'll see why the word *blind* is part of the name of this game.

How to Play:

1. After shuffling, the two to five players draw five dominoes each and arrange their tiles, facedown in a row, long sides touching. The extra dominoes are set aside.

2. Player one turns over the first domino on the left side of his row and plays it, faceup, in the center of the table.

3. Player two turns over the first domino on the left side of his row and plays it if either end matches one of the ends of the domino already played. If he cannot make a move, he puts the tile at the right end of his row.

4. The round is over when one player plays all his dominoes or when no one can play. Scoring is determined the usual way.

Variation:

For a longer game, divide as many dominoes as possible equally among the players: Two players draw fourteen dominoes each, three players draw nine, and so on.

United States

Mexican Train Names of games change as they move from country to country, from continent to continent. Mexican Train has been played in Texas for many years, and is also known as Ends. Who made the rules? Who brought the game to Texas? There are some things about this fascinating game that we will never know!

How to Play:

1. After shuffling, the four players each draw seven dominoes.
2. The player with the double-six goes first.
3. Player two must play a domino with six spots on one end. This second domino forms a line, or train, toward player two. She will play on this line on each turn.
4. Player three then starts a train from the side of the double-six facing her. Player four does the same.
5. If a player cannot play, she passes, and the next player may play on that player's train, as well as her own—but not once the player who passed can again play.

6. The round is over when one player plays all her dominoes or when no one can play. Scoring is determined the usual way.
7. In the second round, the first domino played is the double-five. Third round play begins with the double-four, and so on.

Variation:

In a variation of this game, a player who cannot make a match asks the player on her left for a domino. If that player has a matching domino, she must give it up. If she does not have a matching domino, the next player on her left is asked and so on until the first player finds a matching domino. If no one has a matching domino, the first player may play *any* domino in her hand.

Muggins This game, played in many countries, was the one I knew simply as Dominoes when I was growing up in Texas. It's still played from the Gulf Coast to the Panhandle of Texas, and is sometimes called All Fives.

Each player tries to score the most points, and points are earned when the spots at the two ends of the line add up to five or multiples of five. In All Threes, the point count is based on multiples of three, and in Threes and Fives, it's based on multiples of three and multiples of five.

How to Play:

1. Shuffle the dominoes. If two play, each draws seven; for three or four, each draws five.

2. The player with the highest double goes first. If this is a double-five, player one scores ten points.

3. Player two must match one end of the double or draw. Every time a player plays a domino that results in the ends of the line having a total of five spots, or a multiple of five, he scores five points. For instance, if player two adds a five-blank to the opening double-five, he scores five points (0 + 5 = 5).

4. Doubles are played across the line, and the spots on both ends of the double are counted.

5. The round is over when one player plays all his dominoes or when no one can play. Scoring at the end of the round is determined the usual way. This game is often played up to two hundred points.

29

Vietnam

Vietnamese Dominoes

Vietnam, in Southeast Asia, is shaped like a long stretched letter S. In the north, the top touches China, then the country twists and curves around Laos and Cambodia. The South China Sea washes against Vietnam's coastline. Following decades of war, North Vietnam and South Vietnam were reunited in 1976 as the Socialist Republic of Vietnam.

Vietnamese of all ages play a noisy game of dominoes. Set outside or on a porch, the table must be strong, because dominoes are sometimes thrown or slammed as they are played. Usually four people play, either as partners or individuals. Adults often hold their dominoes in their hands.

How to Play:

1. All the players shuffle the dominoes, and each draws one domino.

2. If no one draws the double-six the first time, players continue to draw until someone finds it.

3. The players reshuffle all of the dominoes and arrange them, dots down, in two or three lines. The player who drew the double-six places a domino crosswise on whichever line she chooses. Hanging off the end of a line, this domino is called the tail.

4. Beginning from a line without a tail, each player chooses one domino at a time until the last domino, the tail, is reached. The tail goes to the winner of the double-six draw.

5. The player who drew the double-six this time now slams it to the middle of the table to start the next part of the game.

6. Play continues with lines developing from the middle of the double-six, not the ends. A player must match one end of the lines or draw. If a double is played, it is played across the line, but new lines do not develop from the ends of the double.

7. The round is over when one player plays all her dominoes for a score of zero, or when no one can play. Each player receives as her score the count of the unplayed dominoes remaining in her hand.

8. If a player is left with the double-blank, she gets thirteen points.

9. When one player reaches fifty points, the game is over. The winner is the player with the lowest score.

Dominoes for One Player

Solitaire

Solitaire is a French word that means "by yourself." The game is not difficult to learn, and it will help you remember number combinations that equal twelve. Domino Solitaire is also called Domino Dozen.

How to Play:

1. After shuffling, draw six tiles and arrange them, faceup, side by side, in a line in front of you. This line is called a tableau, or picture. It will look like this.

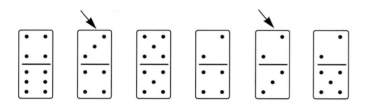

2. If all the spots on two dominoes in the tableau total twelve, put those tiles in the boneyard. For instance, a three-four and a two-three would be discarded.

3. Draw two more dominoes from the boneyard to replace those discarded. Again, discard two dominoes totaling twelve. Continue to draw and discard, checking to see if you can eliminate more than one pair at a time.

4. If you end up without two dominoes that total twelve, you lose.

Variations: Grace's Patience and Fair Lucy

Patience is another name for Solitaire. It does take patience to play both these games. The name Grace's Patience may have come from this English rhyme:

> *Patience is a virtue,*
> *Virtue is a grace.*
> *Grace is a naughty girl*
> *Who wouldn't wash her face!*

How to Play Grace's Patience:

1. Shuffle the dominoes, arranging all twenty-eight facedown in a straight line, long end to long end.

2. Turn each domino faceup, maintaining the end-to-end line, and discard any two that have the same number of spots on *joining* ends.

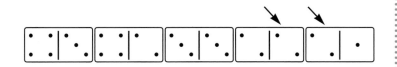

3. Continue to turn dominoes over and, as you discard, move the remaining dominoes together so

that you always have a straight line of touching dominoes.

4. If you discard all twenty-eight dominoes, you win. Don't be discouraged if this doesn't happen very often.

How to Play Fair Lucy:

1. Shuffle the dominoes and arrange seven of them facedown in a straight line.

2. Put a second row, facedown, on top of the first. The third row goes facedown on top of the second. Place the fourth, and last, row faceup.

3. Discard any two faceup dominoes that have spots totaling twelve. As you remove dominoes, turn over the dominoes that you have uncovered.

4. When you remove the bottom piece from a pile, leave the space empty. Do not move a piece from another pile to the space.

5. Continue until you have discarded all dominoes. If you do, you win. If you can no longer play, you lose and must begin again if you wish to continue playing.

Puzzle #1

In any domino set, the four dominoes that have the lowest number of spots are the double-blank, blank-one, blank-two, and one-one. Following the pattern below, arrange these four dominoes so that each side of the square they form has a total of two spots.

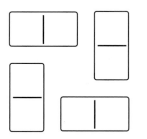

Once you figure this puzzle out, you'll be ready for the more challenging one on the right. And if you get stuck, the answers are on page 36.

Puzzle #2

Separate the following dominoes from the set—the blank-one, blank-two, blank-three, one-one, one-two, one-three, two-two, two-three, and three-three. Following the pattern below, arrange four of the dominoes so that each side of the square has the same number of spots.

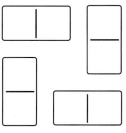

You can place these dominoes in the square pattern so that each side of the square will total three, four, five, six, or seven!

Answers

Puzzle #1

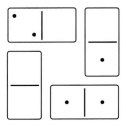

All sides add up to two.

Puzzle #2

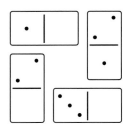

All sides add up to three.

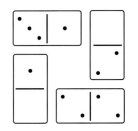

All sides add up to four.

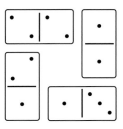

All sides add up to five.

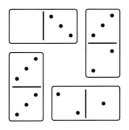

All sides add up to six.

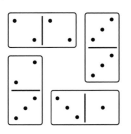

All sides add up to seven.

Delectable Disappearing Dominoes

Making these dominoes will help you become more aware of domino number patterns and give you practice adding and subtracting. Best of all, you can eat these dominoes!

Materials needed:
a set of standard double-six dominoes
  for reference
1 package of graham crackers
1 jar of smooth peanut butter
table knives, 1 for each person
pretzel sticks
raisins, round candy,
  or circle-shaped cereal pieces

Before making Delectable Disappearing Dominoes, cover tables or desktops with paper. Then evenly distribute the *real* dominoes to each person. Note the dividing line across each domino.

Look at the spot patterns on each end. The patterns are always the same.

The number one is always represented by one spot, in the center.

The number two, represented by two spots, always has one spot in the upper left corner and the other in the lower right corner.

The three spots representing the number three always appear in the same pattern, one in the upper left corner, one in the center, and one in the lower right corner.

The four spots for number four are always found at the four corners.

The five spots for number five always appear in the four corners and in the center.

The six spots for number six always form two rows of three spots each along the sides.

Now that you have studied the spot patterns, you are ready to begin to make Delectable Disappearing Dominoes. Each person must have one graham cracker, one spreading knife, a small cup of peanut butter, and a supply of pretzel sticks and circle shapes (raisins, candy, or cereal).

1. Spread peanut butter on one side of graham cracker.

2. Use a pretzel stick to make a dividing line.

3. Add circle shapes on each end of the domino to represent numbers. The numbers on each end might add up to your age on your next birthday. You decide!

Domino Dictionary

blocked: When players can no longer play and cannot draw from the boneyard, the game is blocked.

boneyard: Dominoes remaining after players have drawn.

deck: Another name for a set of dominoes.

Domino: The first player to play all of his or her dominoes, or go out, calls "Domino!"

double: A domino with the same number of spots, or a blank, on each end.

draw: Each player draws, or takes, a certain number of dominoes to play a game. In some games dominoes are also drawn from the boneyard.

face: The side of the dominoes with spots, blanks, or a combination.

line: The row of dominoes as they are played, end to end.

match: In most games players must match the spots on one end of a domino (or row of dominoes) already on the table with the spots on the end of a domino they wish to play.

pass: When necessary, a player may state that he cannot play. His turn passes to the next player.

set: In double-six dominoes, the twenty-eight tiles, or individual dominoes, needed for play. There are also double-nine sets and double-twelve sets.

shuffle: To move the dominoes, facedown, on the table to mix them before players draw the number required for the game.

spinner: The first domino played in a game. Most games require that this be the highest double held by one of the players.

spots: The circles on the ends of dominoes, also called pips.

tile: A domino playing piece, also called domino, bone, stone, and man.

Bibliography

Describing some of the resources that I used in writing about dominoes provides clues about interesting places to visit in search of information on any topic: I viewed documents on a microfiche reader, communicated via E-mail, visited web sites, and conducted interviews, in person and on the telephone; I also used our public library facilities and interlibrary loan to receive faxed copies of articles. I am always delighted when I learn new facts. Sometimes these facts don't relate directly to the subject being researched. This is always the author's dilemma—staying on task and completing the project! I hope these resources inspire you to search for other books on the subject of dominoes and related topics. Better yet, I hope they help you expand your fun with dominoes.

Armanino, Dominic C. *Dominoes: Games, Rules, and Strategy.* New York: Simon & Schuster, 1977.

Armanino, Dominic C. *Dominoes: Five Up and Other Games.* New York: David McKay, 1980.

Belton, John, and Joella Cramblit. *Domino Games.* Milwaukee, Wisconsin: Raintree Children's Books, 1976.

Bernardi, Anita. *Games from Many Lands.* Scarsdale, New York: Lion Press, 1970.

Berndt, Fredrick. *The Domino Book: Games, Solitaire, Puzzles.* Nashville, Tennessee: Thomas Nelson, 1974.

Botermans, Jack. *The World of Games: Their Origins and History, How to Play Them, and How to Make Them.* New York: Facts on File, 1987.

Brandreth, Gyles. *Domino Games and Puzzles.* London: Transworld, 1975.

Cassell's Complete Book of Sports and Pastimes: Being a Compendium of Outdoor and Indoor Amusements. London: Cassell, 1896.

Culin, Stewart. *Korean Games: With Notes on the Corresponding Games of China and Japan.* New York: Dover, 1991.

David, F. N. *Games, Gods, and Gambling.* London: C. Griffin, 1962.

Endrei, Walter, and Laszlo Zolnay. *Fun and Games in Old Europe.* Budapest, Hungary: Corvina Books, 1986.

Gronert, Joie, and Sally Marshall. *Math Starring the Dominoes: Activities Using Dominoes Designed to Reinforce Basic Facts and to Stimulate Strategic Thinking for Problem Solving.* Des Moines, Iowa: Elementary Mathematics Program, 1979.

Grunfeld, Frederic V., editor. *Games of the World: How to Make Them, How to Play Them, How They Came to Be.* New York: Holt, 1975.

Leeflang, K. W. H. *Domino Games and Domino Puzzles.* Translated by Irene Cumming Kleeberg. London: Hamlyn, 1976.

Mohr, Merilyn Simonds. *The Games Treasury: More Than 300 Indoor and Outdoor Favorites with Strategies, Rules, and Traditions.* Shelburne, Vermont: Chapters Publishing, 1993.

Pick, J. B. *Dictionary of Games.* London: J. M. Dent, 1952.

Sackson, Sid. *A Gamut of Games.* New York: Castle Books, 1969.

Speca, Bob, Jr. "The Domino Effect." *Houston Chronicle,* February 20, 1994.

Vinton, Iris. *The Folkway Omnibus of Child Games.* Harrisburg, Pennsylvania: Hawthorn Books, n.d.

And be sure to visit the following dominoes site on the World Wide Web: http://www.princeton.edu/~accion/domino.html.

Index

"across the line"

    definition of, 16

    instances of, 16, 20

All Fives (United States), 28

All Sevens (Spain), 20

Bergen (the Netherlands), 18

Billiton (United States), 24

blank, definition of, 8

Blind Dominoes (United States), 24

Blind Hughie (United States), 24

blocked game, 11, 38

bone, 6, 7, 8, 38

bonepile, 10

boneyard, 10, 38

Cuba, 12

domino

    fundamentals, 10–11

    glossary, 38

    origins, 6–7

    puzzles, 35–36

    solitaire games, 32, 34

Domino Dozen, 32

double, 8, 38

double-nine dominoes, 8, 38

double-six dominoes, 8, 38

double-twelve dominoes, 8, 38

drawing tiles, 10, 38

edible dominoes, 37

Ends (United States), 26

Fair Lucy, 34

France, 14

French Draw, 14

glossary, 38

Grace's Patience, 34

Holland, 18

Kwat P'ai, 6

Mah-jongg, 6

Malta, 16

Maltese Cross, 16

Matador (Spain), 20

Mexican Train (United States), 26

Muggins (United States), 28

Netherlands, the, 18

passing, 38

play, fundamentals of, 10–11

puzzles, 35–36

Russian Dominoes (Spain), 20

scoring, 11

shuffling, 10, 38

solitaire games, 32, 34

Spain, 20

strategy, 11

suits, 8

terms, 38

Texas, 6, 26, 28

tiles, 8, 38

Tutankhamen, King, 6

Ukraine, 22

understanding the pieces, 8

United States

    Blind Hughie, 24

    Mexican Train, 26

    Muggins, 28

Vietnam, 30

who goes first, 10